Mona's Dreams

"You, LORD, preserve both people and animals. How priceless is your
unfailing love, O God! People take from your river of delights."
                                                    —Psalm 36:6-8, NIV

Stewart G. Young, ><>, USMC, MD

WestBow Press books may be ordered through booksellers or by contacting:

WestBow Press
A Division of Thomas Nelson & Zondervan
1663 Liberty Drive
Bloomington, IN 47403
www.westbowpress.com
1 (866) 928-1240

Because of the dynamic nature of the Internet, any web addresses or links contained in this book may have changed since publication and may no longer be valid. The views expressed in this work are solely those of the author and do not necessarily reflect the views of the publisher, and the publisher hereby disclaims any responsibility for them.

Any people depicted in stock imagery provided by Getty Images are models, and such images are being used for illustrative purposes only.
Certain stock imagery © Getty Images.

Interior Image Credit: Harold Branham

Scripture quotations marked (NIV) are taken from the Holy Bible, New International Version®, NIV®. Copyright © 1973, 1978, 1984, 2011 by Biblica, Inc.™ Used by permission of Zondervan. All rights reserved worldwide. www.zondervan.com The "NIV" and "New International Version" are trademarks registered in the United States Patent and Trademark Office by Biblica, Inc.™

Scripture taken from the New King James Version®. Copyright © 1982 by Thomas Nelson. Used by permission. All rights reserved.

ISBN: 978-1-9736-8568-5 (sc)
ISBN: 978-1-9736-8569-2 (e)

Library of Congress Control Number: 2020902629

Print information available on the last page.

WestBow Press rev. date: 03/16/2020

DEDICATION

"If anybody understands God's ardor for his children, it's someone who has rescued an orphan from despair, for that is what God has done for us."

—Max Lucado (The Great House of God)

In light of God's view of adoption, most especially for People, who, as it turns out, are the *real* Bad Dogs; and, of His love for all of His Creation – most particularly, in this case, for the Creatures - this book is dedicated to Him, the Creator and Sustainer of All Things, and Our Father, who art in Heaven.

"God decided in advance to adopt us into his own family by bringing us to himself in Jesus Christ."

—Ephesians 1:5, NLT

"Until he extends the circle of his compassion to all living things, man will not himself find peace."

—Dr. Albert Schweitzer, 1923*

Table of Contents

* Albert Schweitzer Quotes. BrainyQuote.com, BrainyMedia Inc, 2019. https://www. brainyquote.com/quotes/albert_schweitzer_140889, accessed November 21, 2019.

PREFACE

Who knows what dogs are dreaming of when they twitch, run, bark, and "talk" in their sleep? Sure, it's Dog stuff - but, *what*, particularly?

If you know Dogs, you know what they like, which I should think may give some indication about what they dream about:

FOOD: steak-trimmings from the former vegetarian, who is now at least trying to eat less fat, which tasty delight is a natural part of a lucky-dog of a carnivore's diet. Perhaps some nice lasagna, with a bit of antipasto (hold the onions for dogs) left on the plate by a Human whose eyes were bigger than her stomach - a concept unknown to Dogs. Maybe some of Mama's meatloaf drippings drizzled over kibble; Dad's soup that nobody else liked (but, is a *big* hit with the Dogs); strawberries that have outlived their stay in the fridge; raw broccoli – or, even better, collard green stems - and, maybe even raw carrots, if the horses don't get them first; and, of course, bacon!, Bacon!!, BACON!!! As you might guess, little gets wasted around our house; and, with an average of about 10 dogs to share it amongst, nobody gets too much of a good thing, so dogs stay healthy and fit.

But, what *else* do you suppose Dogs dream of besides food?

THE WILD? Howling at the Moon, perhaps? Or, running with the Big Dogs? Maybe chasing Squirrels, running Deer, flushing Birds, or running from Coyotes? Sparring with the Cat - and, prevailing, for once?

MAKING PUPPIES? How about sparkin' with a French Poodle? Or nursing pups? Or, tussling with the youngsters, teaching them Dog-skills?

PROTECTING THE PACK? Could they be repelling Perps and protecting their Pups? Maybe running-off potential competitors for their mate?

I try never to interrupt Dog Dreams – there is something Holy about them. Although, their dreams interrupt my sleep fairly regularly, especially if there is running and barking involved ... which never seems to wake *them* up!

It's always fascinating to lie there, imagining what a particular dog might be imagining in his or her sleep.

Speaking of which, are boy dog dreams different from girl dog dreams?

Do Dogs ever dream of falling? Or, of going to school without their clothes on? Or, of being able neither to run nor walk, move nor speak, nor complete all of the tasks necessary to get out of a dream?

So, into the mist of mystery regarding the nocturnal reveries and phantasms of *Canis lupus familiaris* we shall go, with the help of one Greyhound mix named "Mona", a real dog, now departed but not forgotten, who is doing her thing in Dog Heaven[1], where every Dog's dreams come true. And, with a bit of human imagination.

"Our task must be to free ourselves from this prison by widening our circle of compassion to embrace all living creatures and the whole of nature and its beauty"
—Albert Einstein[2]

---

[1] "Dog Heaven"; Cynthia Rylant; Blue Sky Press; 1995
[2] Albert Einstein. In a letter to bereaved father, Norman Salit. AEA 61-226 March 4 1950. With permission from Chaya Becker of the Albert Einstein Archives.

INTRODUCTION

The Story of Mona:

Mona was a Greyhound Mix who belonged to my daughter, Meghan (now grown and a dog-trainer in her own right), when she was 10-years old and before she was my daughter. She had been pining for a Greyhound, and was advised by her mother, Bobbi, manager of the "Animal Protection League", a no-kill dog & cat shelter in Hopkins, S.C., to look around amongst the 100, or so, dogs housed there to see if there was not something resembling a Greyhound somewhere thereabouts. Whereupon, after a thorough search, Meghan announced with great excitement that she had found one - she had found *Mona*!

Mona ended up in our blended - "recycled", as I call it - family late in life, as the cute red-headed 10-year old Meghan brought her, along with her (Meghan's, not Mona's) 9-year old sister, Kelli, and Kelli's adopted Chihuahua, Reedy (aka "Little Mommy"), when I married their Mother, Bobbi, with her "Nickle Mutt", Mora, the German Shepherd, on the 4th of July, 1999 aboard "Miss Ocracoke", our favorite fishing boat, of a beautiful Sunday morn, on Silver Lake, at Ocracoke Island, N.C., Blackbeard the Pirate's old hang-out, our favorite place, and hence, the perfect event venue for our motley crew.

Not to make too fine a point of it, but I guess you could say Mona got adopted twice!

In return, all of those girls got me, Buzz Braveheart the Jack Russell, and Spike the Bold the American Bulldog.

Shortly after marrying Bobbi, I adopted Meghan and Kelli, who now have S.C. birth certificates attesting to my Fatherhood. Adoption is one of God's specialties, and an important quality for us to emulate in our lives - with both people and animals, officially or unofficially.

Adoption is a part of our stewardship of the Earth, which responsibility was first charged to Adam and Eve.

As I write this, we have 10 dogs and 2 cats in the house (not counting visitors, boarders, slumber-partiers, & transients); and, 4 horses in the yard. Most all of these creatures were adopted, via rescue, and other means. Even Blackbeard had a cat – although it was more likely stolen, than rescued. (Search for "Blackbeard's Cat." His name is Chester.)

Mona was long & lanky, like a Greyhound, if a bit shorter in stature than the tall leggy sort of Greyhound whom you might be familiar with; and, she had a shaggy black coat, very unlike the short coat of a greyhound.

When I met Mona, she was already old, somewhat deaf, partly blind, and had a grey muzzle.

Just as it has been for every greyhound I have ever seen, walking was an awkward activity for Mona. But, if you've ever seen a greyhound run, there is nothing awkward about *that*! However, due to her age, Mona did not run like a racing Greyhound, but rather limped like a peg-legged pirate, whether walking or doing her version of running.

She barked like a seal, one "Orf!" at a time, at whatever or whomever it was she could not see, hear, or smell very well, but which whatever or whomever needed to be barked at, the necessity of something or someone actually being there, being neither here nor there, as far as she was concerned.

I never saw Mona in full-pursuit mode when she was awake, because she had lost a couple of steps, to say the least; but, I know she ran fast in her dreams, because I saw her!

So, in memory of sweet Mona, I offer this impassioned, light-hearted, imaginary perambulation into what might have been Mona's somnambulations - "Mona's Dreams."

—*The Dogfather*
Aka: Stewart G. Young, ><>, USMC, MD

CHAPTER 1

Wolfen Dreams:

Whether Mona and her *Canis lupus familiaris* littermates were born in the wild, as Legend has it, or no, I know not; but, I like to imagine Mona having been born and raised in the wooded hills of our little town of Blythewood, in the Midlands of S.C. – an area of the state also known as the Sandhills because it was "The Beach" about 20,000,000 years ago. Many of our hills hereabouts are sand dunes with a veneer of vegetation.

Here, amongst the many springs, streams, and ponds, along with the native deer and turkeys, and Johnny-come-lately western coyotes, may well be where Mona was born and spent her puppyhood.

Western coyotes (*Canis latran*) are small wolves, and are Mona's dog (*Canis*) relatives, that have found their way out of the American West, and expanded their range over most of North America, much to the chagrin of South Carolina deer hunters and cat owners. Ironically, this expansion may be due to another invasive species, non-Native-American human hunters, who killed-off Mona's native South Carolina relatives, the Eastern Wolves [*Canis lupus lycaon*] and Red Wolves [*Canis rufus*]), which species had made the place inhospitable to coyotes.

The Buffalo, or Bison (*Bison bison*), which also used to graze South Carolina's Piedmont Prairies and Midlands are also gone because of those same non-native hunters.

In contrast, the arrowheads found in our pastures and paddocks date back perhaps 6,000 years, when these animals were present, and the native hunters of those days used conservation practices that ensured the survival of the native species that provided them with food, clothing, shelter, bedding, tools, and fuel for the fire, as well as maintaining the Balance of Nature, in general. While some things in our environment are beyond our control, many more are not.

By the time I met her, Mona had a grey muzzle, and a bit of a limp. She did not appear to be much of a hunter, had a Buffalo even been available; but, to be fair, I did not know her precise history ... nor, her dreams!

She had that far-away look in her eyes commonly seen in greyhounds, and possessed their typical quietly-standing-about-waiting-for-something-to-chase look, both of which might be mistaken for a lack of intelligence by those used to such quick studies as Jack Russells, German Shepherds, Wolves, or Coyotes.

When she barked her seal-bark "Orf!", she often emphasized it with a little front-end bouncy thing which, considering her arthritis, added a bit more comedy to the whole affair, and was anything but fearsome.

We used to take her along with our various other dogs on "hunts" (i.e., walkies) in the woods behind our neighborhood, which may have had a familiar scent to her, and may have had held buffalo and wolf bones beneath our feet.

At the time, her Pack consisted of Reedy the Chihuahua, Mora the German Shepherd, Buzz the Jack Russell, and Spike the American Bulldog, all of whom are now on walkies in Dog Heaven with her.

Much of those woods are now vinyl-sided haunts of dogs for whom the now-defunct moniker *Canis domesticus* might warrant revival. However, I have no doubt that all of those dogs would love to have roamed the woods with our congenial mixed pack, and no doubt enjoyed dog dreams of their own.

CHAPTER 2

Puppy Dreams:

Even though we have no particular information about Mona's parents or her puppyhood, nor did we ever meet any of her siblings, we do know that puppies stir-up their own share of mischief, starting for Mona, perhaps, when that rascally black lab-chow mix "dirty dog" of a father ran off, which is pretty natural for dogs.

Whether sweet old Mona was ever party to any mischief herself is hard to say; however, she was a dog, and as everyone knows, dogs are inclined to run. Surely, she tussled with her littermates, stimulating the development of her nerves, muscles, bones, sinews, and cunning; and, developing physical skills, putting it all together into the Dog's Dance.

There are plenty of rabbits hereabouts, and I should think not a few of them were put to flight by the pups.

If she chased pickup trucks down dirt roads, she apparently had the sense not to catch one; or, if she ever did, she showed no evidence that she was the worse for wear for the experience.

We don't know if Mona ever had a human family, nor if she ever had puppies of her own.

In any case, these years were not lost to Mona; and, I hope she was able to have all the dreams every adolescent shares, coming of age!

CHAPTER 3

Adoption Dreams:

When, or even *if*, Mona was lost, she was, at some point, *found*, and took up residence at The Animal Protection League (APL) in Hopkins, S.C. a no-kill dog and cat shelter. The disposition of her Father, Mother, and Siblings will always, it seems, remain a mystery.

It was in my following-up on a brood of feral puppies born in the woods of a different feral mother who had hung around during the construction of a Columbia neighborhood where I had lived previously, which mother and pups ended up at the APL, that I met Bobbi, Meghan, & Kelli, Mora, Reedy, and, of course, Mona.

This other feral mother, given the name "Nellie", would never let me pet her, either at the house where she would eat at a distance (and, thereby become healthy enough to breed), or in the fenced pen at the APL where she raised her *very* active puppies.

She would allow me, however, to enter the pen to play with (that is, get shredded by) her enthusiastic semi-feral youngsters, all of whom went to good homes, as did their skittish mother, which was all a work of Divine Adoption, to be sure.

Mona was one of perhaps 100 dogs in pens, runs, and various sorts of in/outdoor arrangements at the Animal Protection League, while the cats had the luxury of their own house. Whenever anyone would walk into the main building or stroll by the various pens and runs, the dogs would light-up, barking and running about.

I always liked this rowdiness, perhaps because it was, for me, the domesticated version of a wolfpack in full song. For the same reason, I like it when our household erupts with song when I get home, with the full range of a pipe organ, from Chihuahuas to the Big Dogs. I get the same pleasure when I hear the Coyotes in song in the woods across the street, or the foxes out back in our woods. There is something primordial about the whole affair; something beyond domestication – mine, or theirs.

Prior to meeting Mona, Meghan had adopted an "oldie" named "Shemona", who straightaway became quite ill with cancer and headed for Dog Heaven shortly thereafter, leaving Meghan heart-broken.

Meghan had always wanted a greyhound, so Bobbi sent her into Deepest Dogdom at the Animal Protection League to see if there might be a greyhound mix in there, somewhere.

Indeed, there was! The long-desired greyhound mix was found, adopted, and named "Mona".

There may have been an understandable bit of apprehension on Meghan's part, due to Mona's age and her previous heart-breaking experience with Shemona, but fortunately Meghan's and Mona's mutual greyhound adoption dreams were realized, and Mona came home to live with Bobbi, Meghan, Kelli, Mora, Reedy, and their dog-eating Monk Parrot, "Beefy," all together in their single-wide trailer, in Edmund, S.C., in the days before we blended packs.

CHAPTER 4

Hearth & Home Dreams:

When, on the 4th of July, 1999, Bobbi and her entourage joined me and my entourage, we became the reconstituted Young Family, and we all moved into a 50-year old stone farmhouse, made the year I was born, on 3.5 acres in Blythewood, S.C.

We have named the place Snug Harbor.calm, although it is not always snug nor calm, depending on who or what is causing the Disturbance of the Moment:

- UPS delivering;

- a family member arriving - dogs know the sound of their peoples' cars;

- the Hay Guys delivering food for the horses. We now have four horses, two of whom were rescued from a Slaughter Auction in New Jersey. We got two for the price of one, as "Jerzee Gurl" was pregnant with "Dixie", who was born right out in our back yard, under the big oak tree, at about 10 PM, on March 21, 2011, just a few hours before my eldest daughter, Carrie's, birthday. Dixie and Carrie are both named for my maternal Grandmother, who taught me how to work. Then there's "Tuffy" who was bought from family friends; and, "Loki", alleged to be a Russian Arabian, secured for $300, after being listed under "Pets" in our local newspaper – he was essentially rescued from becoming somebody's BBQ, which most of the respondents to the ad seemed interested in "adopting" him for.

- Etcetera; it doesn't take much to get somebody - or, everybody - to light-up with the howling, which has cut many a human nap, and temper, short.

Things aren't always snug or calm with the people either, but Meghan and Kelli made it to adulthood successfully, and we love each other more and more as we all continue to mature. There are plenty of dogs to hug to remind us we are loved, if it ever seems like we aren't.

Unbeknownst to us at the time when we moved to Snug Harbor, Mona seems to have been born and raised somewhere in the Blythewood vicinity. Her exact origins and progenitors are a mystery, but in 1999, when Bobbi first took her to the Blythewood Animal Hospital, Dr. Branson told her that it was quite likely that Mona had been a member of a litter of dogs that had grown-up in Blythewood, as she had treated other members of a clan of Mona's age and appearance.

So, Mona came home - as did we all. Perhaps, a dream come true, all 'round. God is great at this stuff!

15

CHAPTER 5

Scent-Hunting Dreams:

Before so much of her native habitat was lost to residential development, Mona, along with the rest of our pack, used to go on walkies, off-lead, in the woods hereabouts. It was, in fact, the first place I ever saw an owl in the wild. A pleasant creek ran through the middle of it all.

We would have to keep an eye on Mona, because her eyes weren't too good, and neither was her hearing. The same could not be said for her ability to scent.

She would pick-up on something, and wander-off 90° to our route of march, following some scent that nobody else detected, and we would have to holler at her "Mona!! Yoo-Hoo!!"

About half of the time, that didn't work, so someone would have to physically go round her up to rejoin the pack.

These were great times, and surely Mona added them to her dreams.

CHAPTER 6

Racing Dreams:

One spring day we took Mona, Reedy, and Buzz to the Dog-A-Rama at the Historic Camden Revolutionary War Site, with its reproduction Kershaw-Cornwallis House, just like the one that British General Cornwallis had used as his headquarters there, along with earthworks, all of which is the site of an annual reenactment of the battle in which the American Revolutionaries were soundly thrashed. Later, a little north of here, an American victory at Kings Mountain, S.C., sent General Cornwallis further north, ultimately to Yorktown, Virginia, where he surrendered. Orf! Orf! Get 'em, Mona!

This was the same dog festival that Buzz Braveheart, in a previous year, when we were both bachelors, had entered as his first competition. He won five ribbons, including a Blue Ribbon for "trailing". Only, Buzz didn't follow the trail to the lure that had been dragged along the ground, hither and yon, inside one of the earthworks, to be hidden behind a bale of hay. No - he lifted his head, air-scented the bait, and ran straight to it!

In the latter year, Mona, in a remarkable take-off of the "wolf in sheep's clothing" ploy, dressed-up in pink rabbit ears. Racing greyhounds (a dubious practice so far as the welfare of the dogs is concerned) have been chasing artificial rabbits around racetracks for many years, wishing, I should think, for a real rabbit to chase.

Being a greyhound at heart, Mona also found herself involuntarily standing-about sharing a blank look with a group of Greyhound Rescue dogs up for adoption, just as if she had been doing it her whole life! It was Dog Heaven on Earth for her.

I suppose, that night she had some rabbit-chasing, and perhaps even some racing, dreams!

CHAPTER 7

Sighthound Dreams:

Sighthounds hunt by, well, *sight*! Greyhounds are one type of sighthound.

One day, towards the end of Mona's life with us, as we were just returning to the house from "the hunt," in the woods, Mona snatched a fledgling Blue Jay off the ground, under the big oak tree, where Dixie was later born. She rendered the traditional (i.e., instinctive) shake, killing the young bird immediately.

We were stunned that she could sense prey - presumably by sight - and act so quickly, when we had neither seen the unfortunate bird, nor had any idea what was happening until it was all over.

Which, I suppose, is the secret to successful hunting.

Dogs are predators, despite their pseudo-domesticated status and scientific name, and their seemingly docile nature when we are rubbing their ears or tummies.

Mona was still a dog! A very *old* dog, but a dog nonetheless, still capable of sight-hunting - and, sight-hunting dreams.

CHAPTER 8

Retirement Dreams:

Mona was old to begin with. I guess she was pretty much retired when we got her. Still, she did what she could to keep up with the pack, even as she got slower, more gimping, and less able to see or hear as time went on.

As people get older, God seems to give them some notion of what is to come, to prepare them for it, and even to welcome it's coming. So, I should think He does the same for dogs, who just seem to be able to be happy being dogs until they are dead.

They don't appear to fret or worry, and don't complain much, even though their arthritis is obvious, or they bump into things or fall down, or can't seem to hear much except "Who wants to eat?"

For Mona, the end came quickly, one December evening before Christmas, when she suddenly became weak and short of breath when trying to come up the few back steps from the dog yard.

I laid with her on a blanket on the mudroom floor, but she waited until I got up and left her alone for a few minutes, to die.

She was the first dog whose passing I experienced, although there have been several – too many - since then (Buzz, Spike, Emmitt, Kayla, Jerry Blue, Louma, Reedy, Mora, Champ, Phatti Patti, Effie, Nonnie, Buster, Baylee, Gigi, and, horses Buddy & Chili, among others). I think Mona helped me to accept the end of life better - for dogs, people, and all of God's Creatures.

I must say that we still have her ashes on the dog room mantle, not ever having been quite sure what to do with them, and somehow comforted by such presence as that is of our sweet Mona.

She surely dreamed of Dog Heaven before she went there, and is now having an eternal dream come true!

CHAPTER 9

Christmas Dreams:

One of my favorite books is "Dogs Think Every Day is Christmas" by Ray Bradbury (best known for his science-fiction works); and, that's because I think every day is Christmas, too!

If dogs really do think that, I suppose that Mona's death shortly before her Humans celebrated Christmas doesn't mean she missed anything, particularly.

Celebrating coming from God, living with God here, and going back to God are probably good things for Humans to consider daily, too, since any number of us will follow Mona before the next Christmas.

"Why wait? Celebrate!", Mona might say, and add:

"And, while you are celebrating Christmas Today, dream about Christmas tomorrow, tonight!"

Thanks, Y'all!

ABOUT MONA:

Mona was old to begin with in 1999, coming as part of the dowry of your author's second wife, Bobbi, along with her two young daughters, Meghan and Kelli. She was, apparently, originally from Blythewood, S.C., although she somehow landed in a no-kill shelter several miles away, the Animal Protection League, in Hopkins, which Bobbi managed. We brought her to Blythewood – to her home, unknowingly – when we moved here that same year. It is thanks to Mona that we have this story. The photo, right to left: Meghan and Mona; Bobbi and Buzz Braveheart (two-time winner of the Camden Dish – there's no "Dish", but he won it twice); and, Kelli with Reedy (aka: "Little Mommy").

ABOUT THE ARTIST:

Harold Branham is the unofficial Blythewood Artist Laureate (pictured with his dog, Henry). He resides here on land that belonged to his granddaddy, and cuts grass for a living despite being in his 8th decade of life – painting & drawing because that's what he likes best. He is oft inclined to just give his works away to folks, knowing that the good Lord will supply his every need – and, does. Henry and three siblings were found by Harold, as puppies, abandoned in a ditch by the road. All found homes, thanks to Harold. Henry is the official greeter at Harold's house.

FURTHER ACKNOWLEDGEMENTS:

First, thank you, Mona, you Sweet Dreamer! Thanks also to my Spirit Guide, whose especiality is giving inspiration and hope where there is otherwise sorrow and anguish. And, finally thanks to all of the patients, friends, and family – particularly, those long-suffering Genteel Readers of the mental meanderings in my random email, "Uh Thaught" – who encouraged me to write. It's amazing how important a brief word can be in encouraging someone.

"Hear our humble prayer, O God, for our friends the animals,
especially for animals who are suffering;
for animals that are overworked, underfed and cruelly treated;
for all wistful creatures in captivity that beat their wings against bars;
for any that are hunted or lost or deserted or frightened or hungry;
for all that must be put death.
We entreat for them all Thy mercy and pity,
and for those who deal with them we ask a heart of compassion
and gentle hands and kindly words.
Make us, ourselves, to be true friends to animals,
and so to share the blessings of the merciful."

— "A Prayer for Animals", Attributed to Dr. Albert Schweitzer[1]

---

[1] "With permission of The Albert Schweitzer Fellowship, Harvard U., Boston, MA."